John Thompson's Modern Course for the Piano — THIRD GRADE

CLASSICAL PIANO SOLOS

20 Original Keyboard Pieces from Baroque to Early 20th Century

COMPILED AND EDITED BY

Philip Low, Sonya Schumann, and Charmaine Siagian

ISBN 978-1-4803-4493-8

WILLIS MUSIC®

EXCLUSIVELY DISTRIBUTED BY

HAL•LEONARD®

Visit Hal Leonard Online at
www.halleonard.com

World headquarters, contact:
Hal Leonard
7777 West Bluemound Road
Milwaukee, WI 53213
Email: info@halleonard.com

In Europe, contact:
Hal Leonard Europe Limited
1 Red Place
London, W1K 6PL
Email: info@halleonardeurope.com

In Australia, contact:
Hal Leonard Australia Pty. Ltd.
4 Lentara Court
Cheltenham, Victoria, 3192 Australia
Email: info@halleonard.com.au

PREFACE

A rarity among piano methods, John Thompson's *Modern Course* was authored by a successful concert artist. For this reason, the pianism found between the pages of the famous "red cover" series corresponds directly with that which is required to play authentic piano literature. A musician of the highest caliber, Thompson (1889–1963) made expert repertoire choices, integrating strong original compositions with accessible arrangements of orchestral and piano classics that perfectly represented the style characteristics of each era, resulting in well-rounded students who could approach any new piece with confidence.

The aim of the *Classical Piano Solos* series is to keep with the spirit of Thompson's repertoire selections by including an assortment of treasured pieces that are taught often and hold status as prized concert music. For example, in the 5th Grade volume are two of the most recognized C-sharp Minor pieces in existence: Beethoven's "Moonlight" sonata and the Rachmaninoff prelude, loved and adored with good reason, yet sometimes unfairly disparaged because of their popularity. (Note that this edition presents the often overwhelming final section of the Rachmaninoff in a more visually accessible layout.) In the same book is Debussy's fast, witty "Doctor Gradus ad Parnassum" and Mozart's D Minor fantasy, unfinished at the time of his death and completed by his student August Eberhard Müller. (Müller's "Lyric Etude" is included in the 1st Grade.) Earlier in the series are other oft-cherished pieces, such as Grieg's spare and wistful "Arietta" and Chopin's intense, evolving "Prelude in E Minor" (both in the 4th Grade), as well as several well-known Bartók miniatures from his 1913 method (1st, 2nd, and 3rd Grade books).

Numerous uncommon treasures were also unearthed, including "A Ghost in the Fireplace" (4th Grade) and "Once Upon a Time There was a Princess" (3rd Grade) from Theodor Kullak's *Scenes from Childhood*, composed for piano students well over a century ago. Though these pieces never quite found their way into published recordings or into the hands of master pianists, for years they provided many students with delightful lesson material as they built their pianistic skills. Other lesser-known gems include works from French composers Mélanie Bonis (*Album pour les tout-petits*, 1st and 2nd Grade) and Cécile Chaminade ("Pièce Romantique," 3rd Grade); Danish composer Ludvig Schytte's Opus 108 (1st and 2nd Grade); Russian composer Anatoly Lyadov's gorgeous, seldom-heard B Minor prelude; and English composer Samuel Coleridge-Taylor's mournful "They Will Not Lend Me a Child," based on a Southeast African folksong about a childless mother (both in the 5th Grade). Quick pieces that dazzle and motivate were intentionally included as well; for example, MacDowell's "Alla Tarantella," C.P.E. Bach's "Presto in C Minor" (both in the 3rd Grade), and Moszkowski's "Tarantelle" (4th Grade).

These authentic piano solos are offered once again in these pages, reconnecting the students of today with beautiful masterpieces from bygone eras.

Correlation with John Thompson's Modern Course. The *Classical Piano Solos* series was compiled to correlate loosely with the *Modern Course* method. The series can be used to supplement any teaching method, but holds its own as a small compendium of advancing piano literature. Worth mentioning is that all the pieces are public domain in the United States, Europe, and around the world. Consequently, no works composed or published after 1920 are included. It is highly recommended that the teacher supplement the lesson with appropriate contemporary literature, including works from outside traditional Western art music, as needed.

Leveling and Layout. Grades 1-4 have been presented in a suggested order of study and progress by approximate level of difficulty. Because of the sophistication and advanced technicality of the pieces in Grade 5, that volume is laid out chronologically, from Baroque to the early 20th Century. Page turns were always a consideration during the engraving and editing process.

Editorial Principles and Sources. When appropriate, occasional articulation, fingerings, and dynamics have been added, especially to pieces from the Baroque and early Classical eras, with the intent of better assisting the advancing performer with an accurate stylistic interpretation. (An exception are fingerings in the Bartók pieces; a few were removed for ease of study.) Urtext sources were consulted whenever available, as well as standard performing editions. The first two pieces in the 1st Grade have been slightly adapted; all other works in the series are originals composed for the keyboard/piano of the time. Compositions without designated titles have been bestowed with fresh ones.

CONTENTS

[Suggested order of study; however, it is recommended that two contrasting works be learned concurrently]

4	The Daring Horseman	GURLITT	Romantic
6	Waltz in B Minor	BARTÓK	Early 20th c.
7	Sad Story	STREABBOG	Romantic
8	Playing Soldiers	REBIKOV	Early 20th c.
10	Once Upon a Time There Was a Princess	KULLAK	Romantic
12	Italian Song	TCHAIKOVSKY	Romantic
14	Ballade	BURGMÜLLER	Romantic
16	Rondo in F Major	HOOK	Classical
18	Shepherd Playing His Pipe	REBIKOV	Early 20th c.
20	Waltz in F Minor	SCHUBERT	Romantic
21	Sonata in G Major	D. SCARLATTI	Baroque
22	Fantasia in C Major	KRIEGER	Baroque
24	Sonatina in C Major	LYNES	Classical-style
30	Scherzo in D Minor	GURLITT	Romantic
32	The Fifers	DANDRIEU	Baroque
34	Rondino in D Major	MOZART	Classical
35	Presto in C Minor	C.P.E. BACH	Baroque-style
38	Alla Tarantella	MacDOWELL	Romantic
42	Prelude in G Major	BACH-SILOTI	Baroque
46	Pièce Romantique	CHAMINADE	Romantic

The Daring Horseman

from *The First Lessons,* Op. 117, No. 32

Cornelius Gurlitt
1820–1901

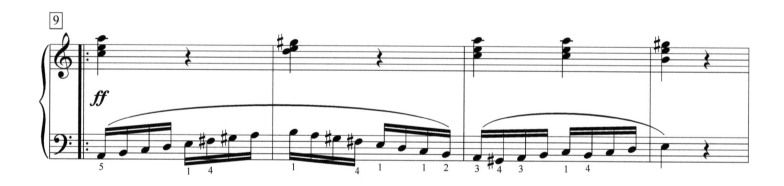

Waltz in B Minor

Béla Bartók
1881–1945

Tempo di Valse

Sad Story

from *12 Very Easy and Melodious Studies,* Op. 63, No. 10

J.L. Streabbog
(Jean Louis Gobbaerts)
1835–1886

Playing Soldiers

from *Silhouettes,* Op. 31, No. 4

Vladimir Rebikov
1866–1920

Strict march time

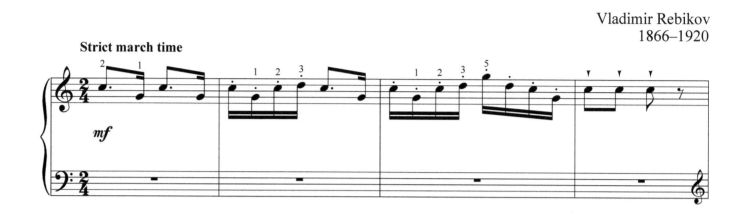

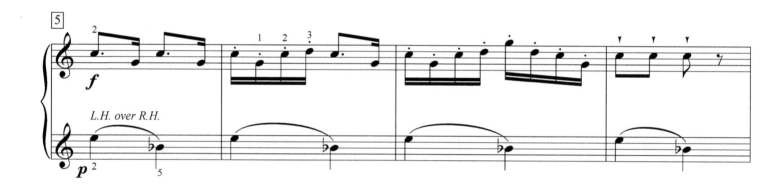

Once Upon a Time There Was a Princess

from *Scenes from Childhood,* Op. 62, No. 1

Theodor Kullak
1818–1882

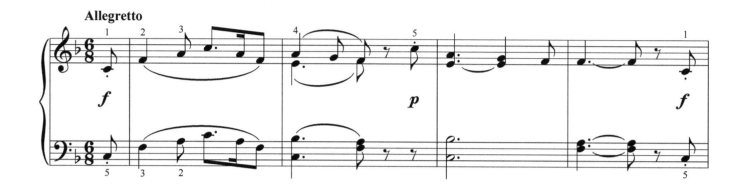

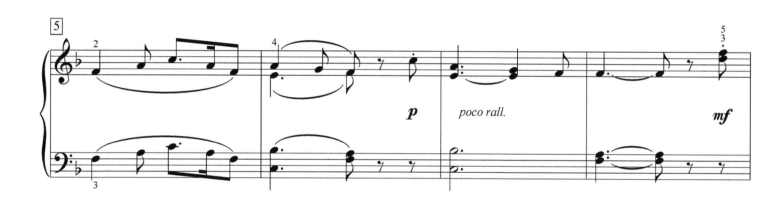

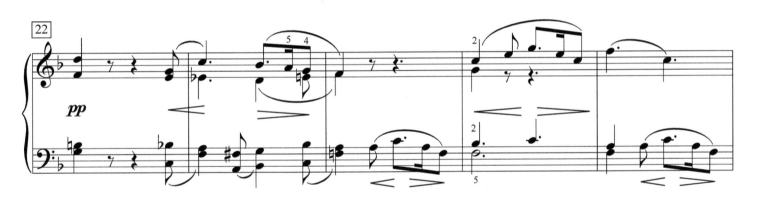

Italian Song

from *Children's Album,* Op. 39, No. 15

Pyotr Il'yich Tchaikovsky
1840–1893

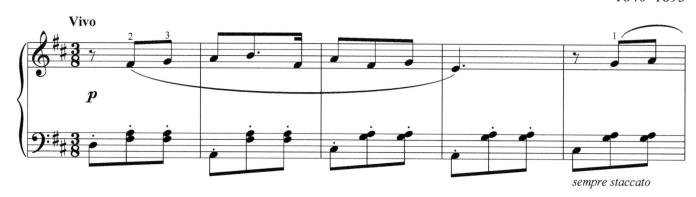

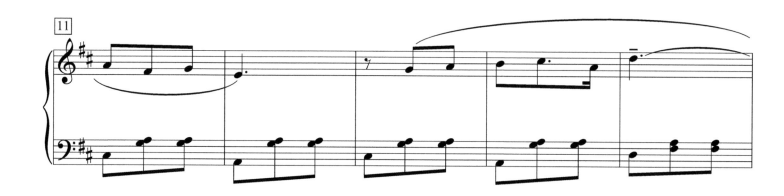

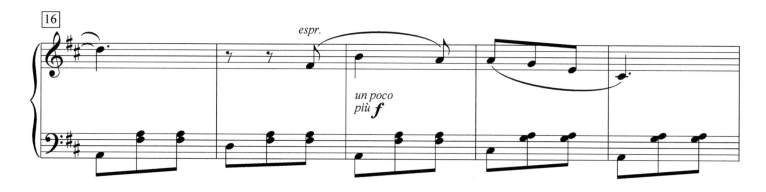

Ballade

from *25 Progressive Etudes,* Op. 100, No. 15

Friedrich Burgmüller
1806–1874

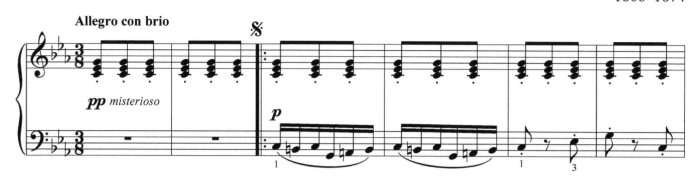

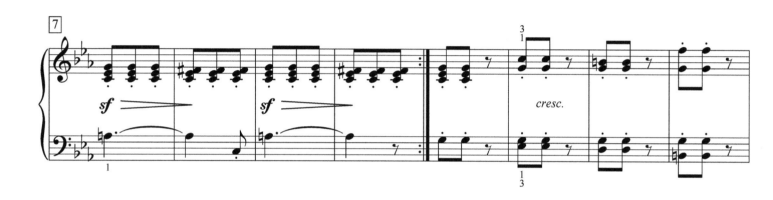

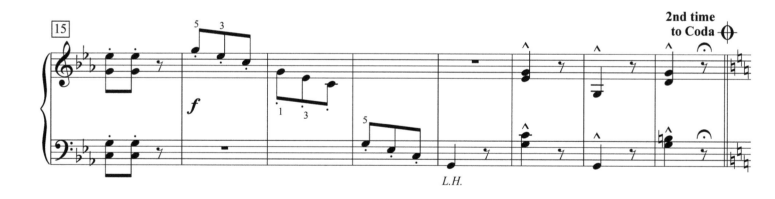

Rondo in F Major

from *Guida di Musica,* Op. 37

James Hook
1746–1827

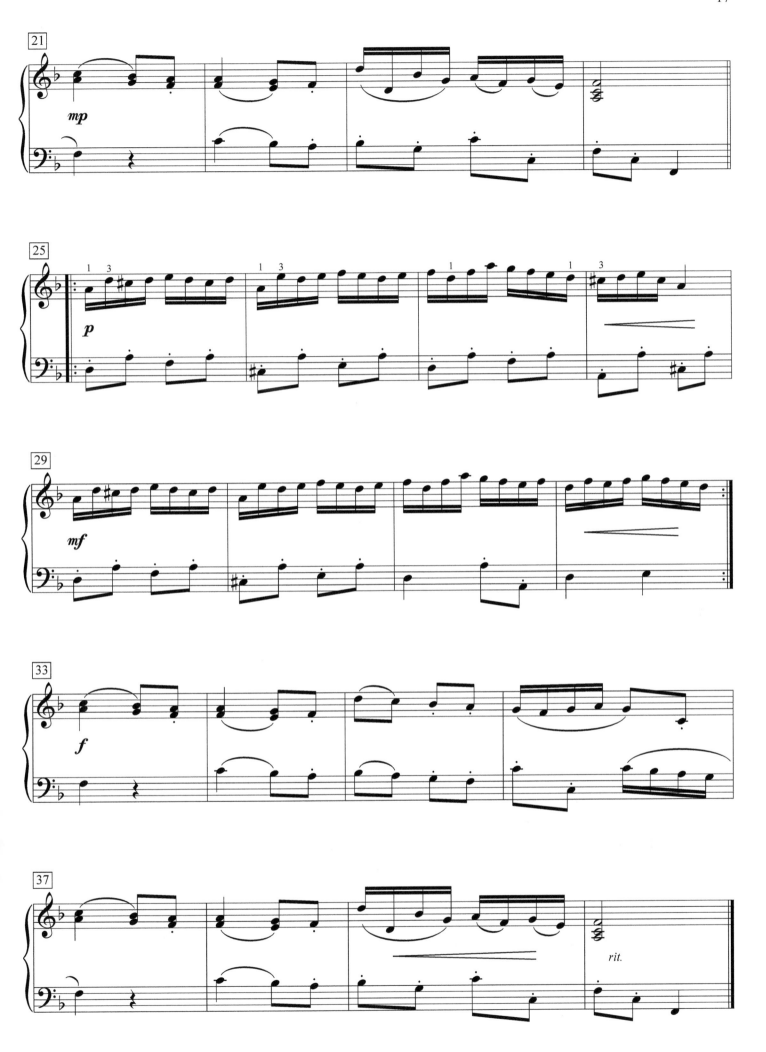

Shepherd Playing His Pipe

from *Silhouettes,* Op. 31, No. 8

Vladimir Rebikov
1866–1920

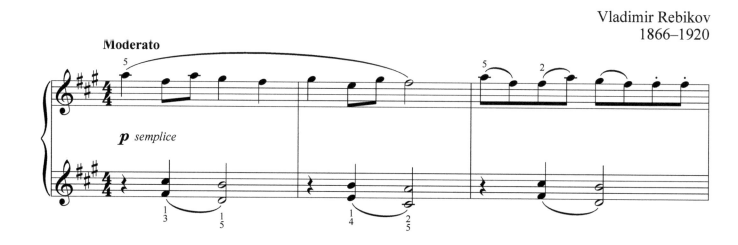

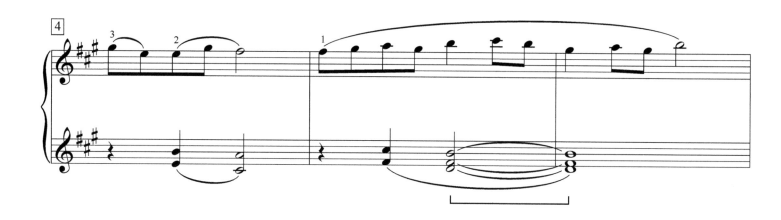

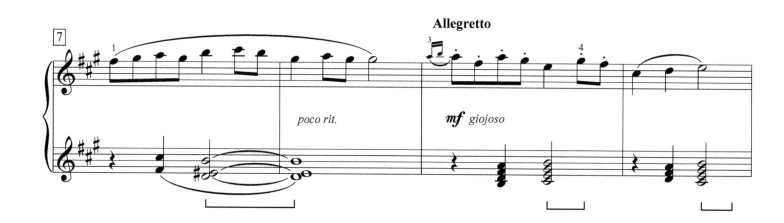

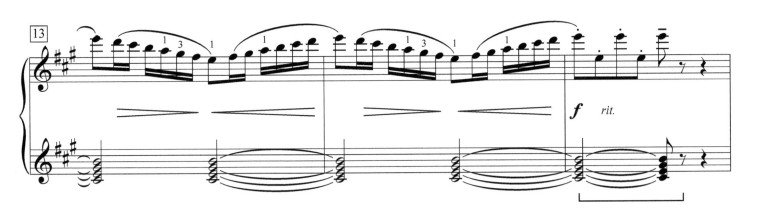

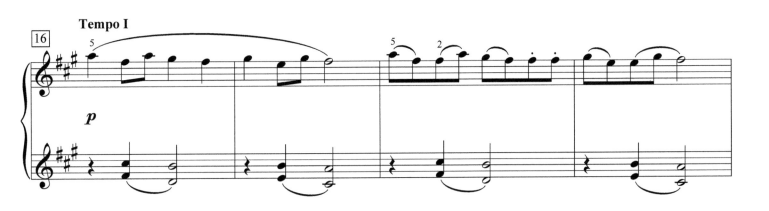

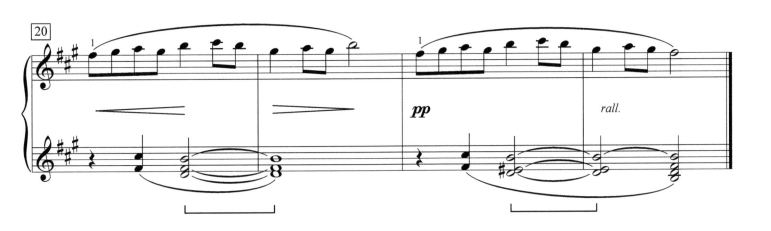

Waltz in F Minor
Op. 33, No. 14 (D. 783)

Franz Schubert
1797–1828

Sonata in G Major

K. 431, L. 83, P. 365

Domenico Scarlatti
1685–1757

Allegro risoluto

Fantasia in C Major

from *Anmuthige Clavier-Übung*

Johann Krieger
1651–1735

Sonatina in C Major
Op. 39, No. 1

Frank Lynes
1858–1913

I. Allegro

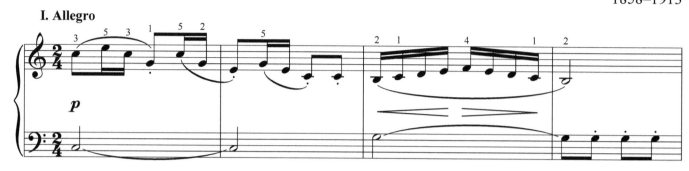

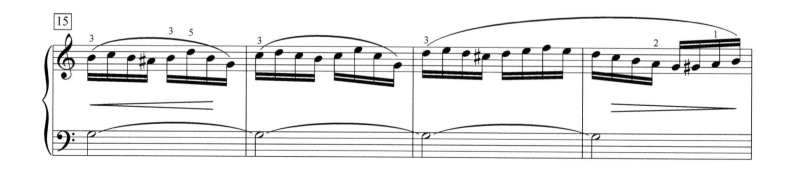

II. Minuet: Allegretto

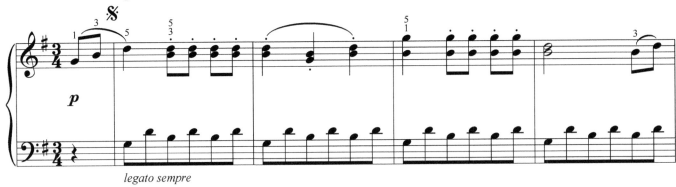

legato sempre

Repeats were eliminated in this movement.

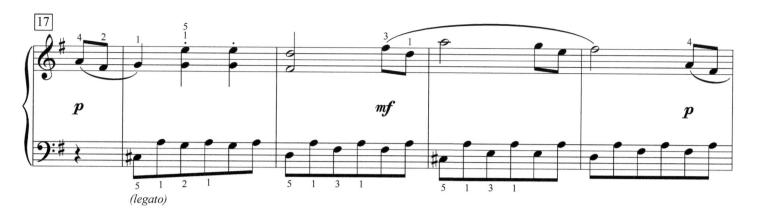

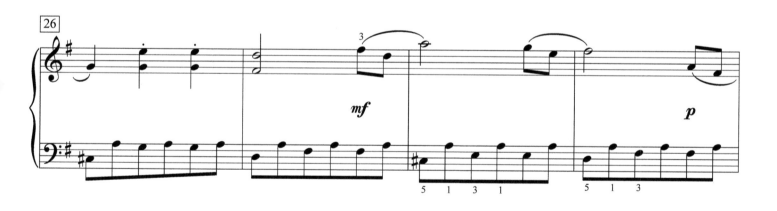

III. Allegro

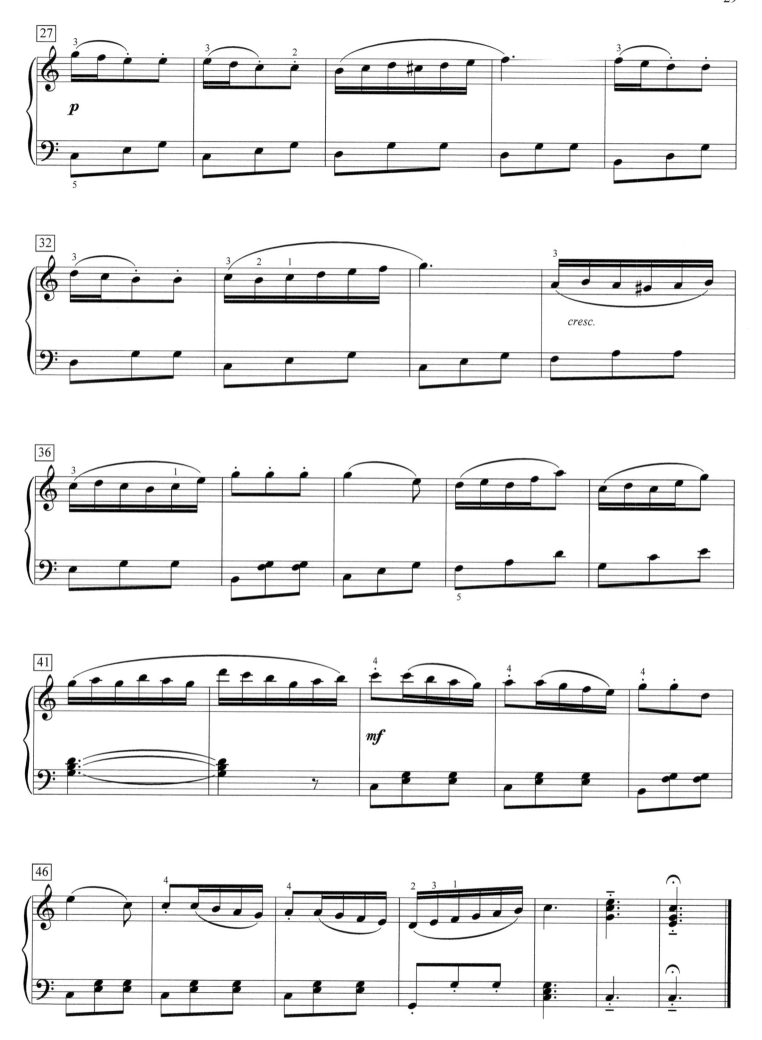

Scherzo in D Minor

Cornelius Gurlitt
1820–1901

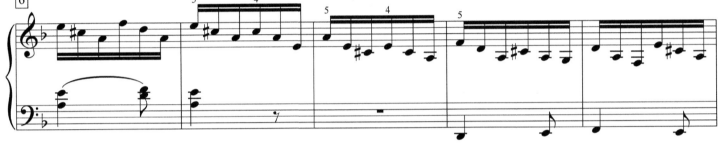

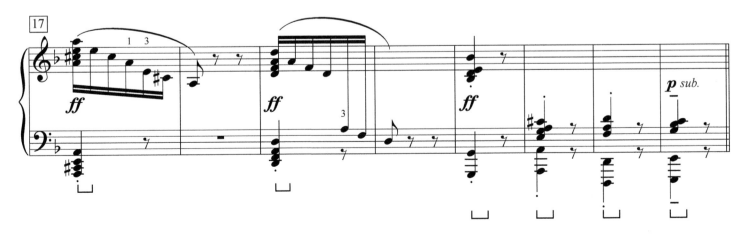

The Fifers

from Suite No. 4, *Pieces de Clavier,* Book 1

Jean-François Dandrieu
1682–1738

Play eighth notes slightly detached.

2nd Couplet

(Back to Rondeau)

D.C. al Fine

Rondino in D Major

from *The London Notebook, KV 15d*

Wolfgang Amadeus Mozart
1756–1791

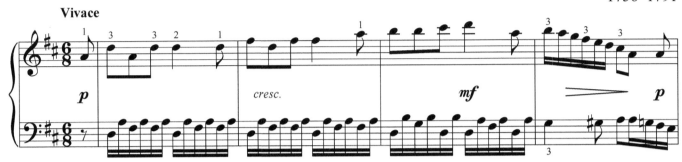

Play eighth notes slightly detached.

Presto in C Minor
Wq. 114/3, H. 230

Carl Philipp Emanuel Bach
1714–1788

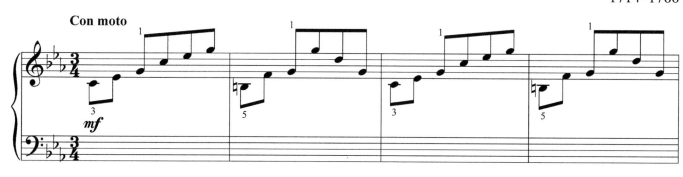

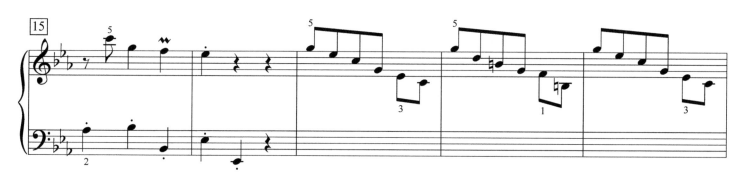

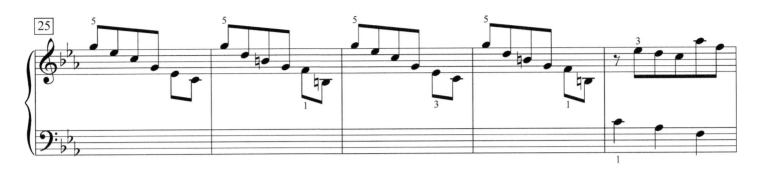

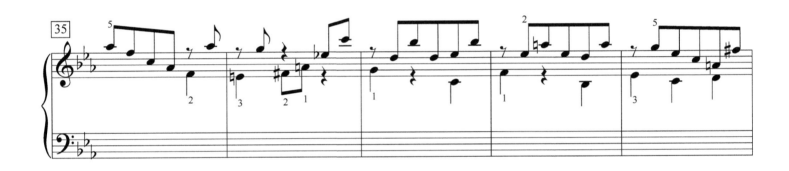

Alla Tarantella

from *12 Etudes,* Op. 39, No. 2

Edward MacDowell
1860–1908

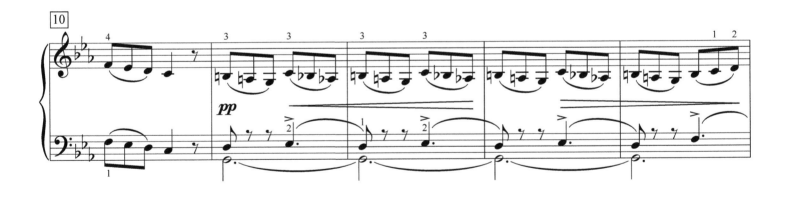

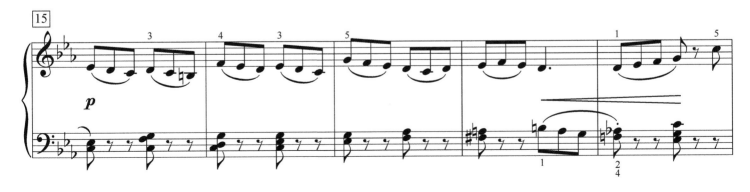

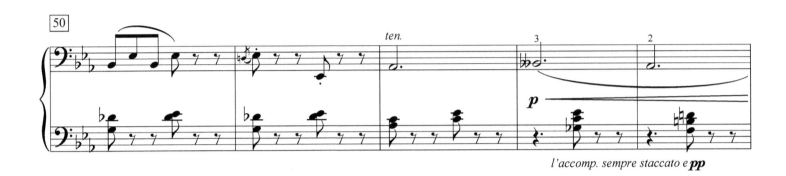

Prelude in G Major

from *Cello Suite No. 1* by J.S. Bach, BWV 1007

Adapted for piano by
Alexander Siloti
1863–1945

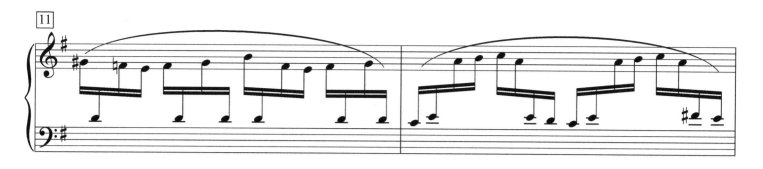

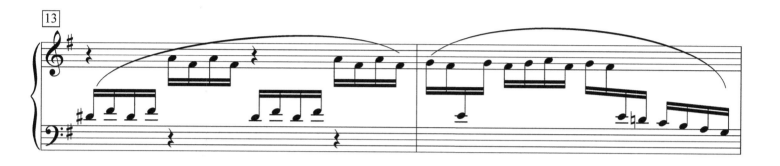

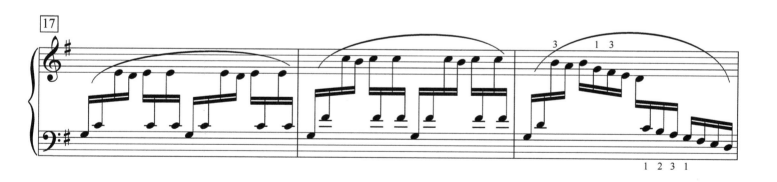

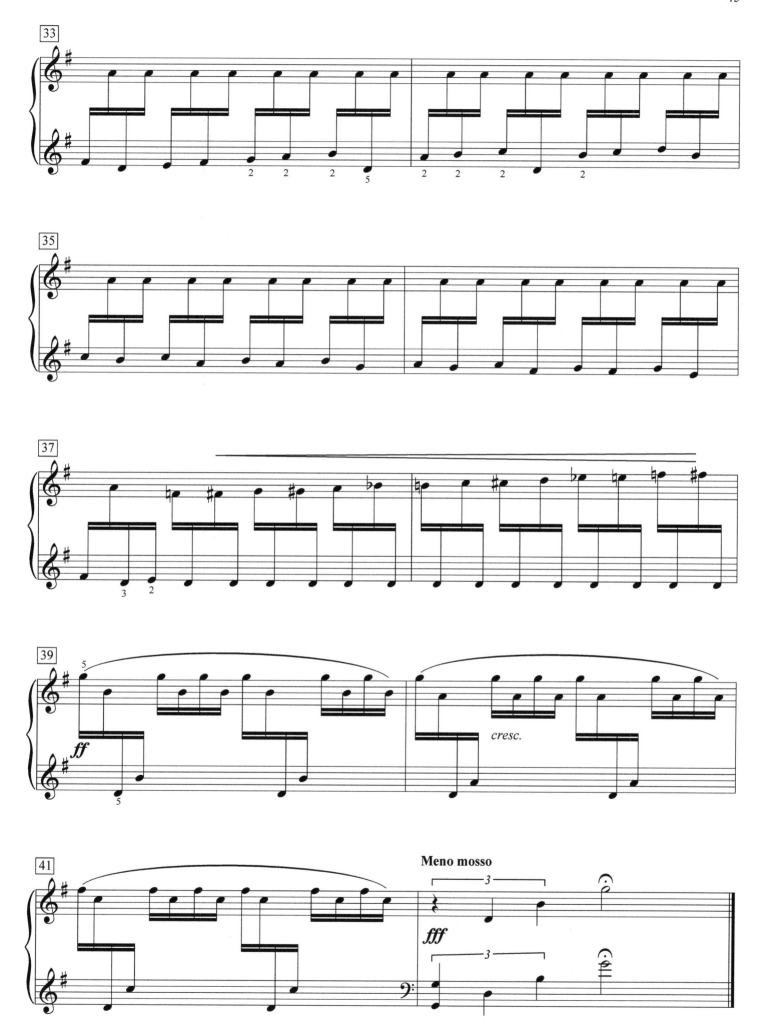

Pièce Romantique

Op. 9, No. 1

Cécile Chaminade
1857–1944

Andante

legato **p** *dolce, ma ben marcato il canto*

dolce

marcato e rit.